Printed in the United States of America

First Printing, 2015

ISBN : 978-0-615-74931-0

www.Amazon.com

I0084997

My Thank You

I would like to thank anyone who took the time to read my writing. It means a lot to me and I appreciate each and every one of you. Also, I would like to thank Team Ayce: Chey, Joe, Melissa, Dirrty, JL, Black, and my Gma. I thank you all for helping me with this book. For all the countless times you had to read and reread my material and helping me edit what flows and what should go. Thank you for all the support and believing in me. I love you and appreciate you all from the bottom of my heart. Thank you so much.

A very special thank you to my baby sister Chey. Even though most times you had no idea, you kept me breathing. I been through hell and back a million times but you gave me that will to fight and be a better person. It's because of you I am still here. All it ever took was that little giggle and big blue eyes. I knew, as long as I had you, nothing in this life would be able to destroy me completely. With all my heart, I love you my lil'princess.

I hope everyone enjoys reading my poems as much as I enjoyed putting this whole thing together. And if my words help someone through a dark time, I could not ask for a better blessing. In closing, just remember every storm runs out of rain. The sun will always find a way to shine.

Ayce

The Silent Reflection

Sitting in the corner, in the dark
Holding my breath, to stop my heart
This time I have fallen too hard
This hell, I knew it wasn't too far
These tears sit silently in my eyes
No one knows the pain I have survived
This love has disintegrated and died
Too much hurt I've held back, with silent cries
It used to be you I trusted
Since your deceit, it's been adjusted
Our gold has been rusted
Our connection is busted
The monster in you wants to tear me apart
While the lover in you wants to mend my heart
These confusing feelings though, keep me sharp
Turning my pain into this art
But we couldn't last
I'll put you on blast
And watch your past
Bite you in the ass
I'm standing right here
With frozen tears
Do you like what you see dear?
When you're looking in the mirror?
So close your eyes, it's you, you fear
If we are not meant to be
I'm not going to force you to be with me
You need your prince charming
And I need to be alone darling
As the sadness starts to show
Years after I have let you go
Don't ask me why I want to be alone
And I won't ask why you need to know

Days end

As I walk this golden shore line
I take a seat on this beach towel of mine
The moist sand sinks between my toes
The warm breeze tickles my nose
In the distance, I hear the squawking of the gulls
Quietly, the day becomes dulled
The gritty taste of the sand lingers on my tongue
While the Lake Erie air fills my lungs
Thoughts from the day dissipate
While the days demise I anticipate
The aroma of old food grease
Bombarded my nostrils from the bars down the street
The bluish green waves make a soft roar
As they unfold onto the reflective lake shore
The sun rays look like an orange carpet of velvet
It makes the illusion that you could walk on it
It's so inviting, it will take me wherever I want to go
Even if it meant traveling to the unknown
Cumulus clouds of puffy blue cotton move in
Closer and closer to the days end

Never forget

My dearest uncle weeny
I can feel you next to me
Whether it's here or there
My car or across the table in a chair
I can talk to you anytime anywhere
I miss you so much I can hardly bare
When I play those old songs
I know you're singing right along
One more time just to feel your warm embrace
Would bring an everlasting smile to my face
But till the day I can see your sweet face again
I will think about memories of you back then
I'll send a kiss to the sky
As a tear falls from my eye
I whisper these meaningful words without further ado
My unk, I love and miss you

Dedicated to: Weeny

Rogue

Your darkness crawls beneath my skin
The misery aches within
I'm infected with your sin
That tainted smile sucks me in
You have raped me of my being
My blood drips from the ceiling
Love, was so crucifying
I lye here, dying
Fractures you have carved in my skull
Chipped away at my brain on every downfall
When I hear the demons call
My sense of strength becomes dulled
You can smell when I bleed
That's when your malevolence will not let me be
Covering my eyes so I'm blind to see
Your devils eating away at me
One kiss plants the ash
I cannot escape our past
My heart fails to heal this gash
From thoughts of our contrast
I'm left feeling like an ass
As I walk away, I hear your evil laugh

My Lil' Princess

As you stood there beautiful in your prom dress,
I soon begin to regress,
Back to the days where I held you as a baby in my arms,
You were my very own lucky charm,
Devoting my life to you and keeping you from harm
My world you definitely are,
Went from changing your diapers,
To putting on your windshield wipers,
Feeding you in a highchair,
Now you're cutting my hair,
Warming the milk in your bottle,
To buying you cans of full throttle
Teaching you your ABC's and 123's
To what the hell is this? Geometry?
Learning the lyrics in my music,
Now you know all the words, and sing loudly to it,
Pushing you around in your little hot wheels car,
Now you have your license and own a car
Giving you piggy back rides around the mall
To you still trying to hop on my back,
forgetting you're now too tall
Kissing your boo's boo's to make em' better,
To breaking your nail in a register,
It's so crazy how fast you grew up
You have definitely grew into a beautiful little
buttercup
Raised you like you were my own,
You have my guarantee I will never
leave you cold and alone
The beauty in life to me you have shown,
If I were to ever lose you , that's something I cannot
condone.

Love going to watch movies with you on the big
screen
Hanging out for hours at the theater, that's just our
thing.
Just so you know if anyone breaks your heart
Send them my way, I won't hesitate to tear them
apart.
Anything you will ever need, you can forever call on
me,
Just keep in mind, no matter where in life we may be,
I love you more than life itself so dearly,
Love forever and always, your big sissy.

Dedicated to: My little sister

The Phantom

As I think of back in the day
When I would beg you to stay
You'd drag me across the floor
To walk out that door
Slamming it in my face
Man my heart would ache
I wouldn't see you for days
There were times I couldn't even concentrate
But I guess you had to feed your selfish ways
Going to get that shit to intoxicate
Always chugging back that beer
Forgetting all that was dear
Your words when you left were always insincere
Getting close you would fear
But these words I hope you hear
I used to hate when the wind blew
That's when I knew
I would turn around
And you were nowhere to be found
Back when I was young, I remember fragments of
you
When you would visit for 5 minutes
then you were off like zoom
I would hug you but smell her perfume
My memories of us seem so gloom
You just didn't care
That I wanted to be anywhere but here
You would play catch with me
But then you would be gone like a breeze
All I wanted was the best of you which was free
You thought all I wanted was a shopping spree
Now you're the one on your knees
Begging me please
Admitting to me you fucked up and I'm like really?
You lost so many years in passing
For some reason you thought my love was ever
lasting
Think again, these scars are so deep
The times you left me to fucking bleed

Shedding tears in front of me, will not get you anywhere
On the real though, go fuck yourself, now that's sincere.

Boogieman

She keeps a firm grip on my ankles,
Her hands are like shackles,
I'm looking all around for the key,
She keeps me in the dark so I cannot see,
She's dragging me along the floor
I keep screaming I can't take anymore
But she pulls me to her for more,
From my eyes, these tears pour.
She makes me addicted to her allure,
Wish this pain I didn't have to endure
Out of breath on this hamster wheel
I'm dodging her bullets without a shield
Her mind is a maze
No way I'm getting out unscathed
It's so dense it's hard to see through the haze
The pain she causes doesn't even phase
I hear her rattle the chains,
It's the summons to get back into my cage
I'm trying so hard to hide in this corner
I just keep wishing to be saved from this horror

California sun

I've never been so ready for a change,
The madness here, has drove me insane,
Wanting to get so far from this place,
Everything I see here stings my eyes like mace.
But I just couldn't wait,
Till I arrived in that state
And got to see the California sun,
It erases all that has been done,
Made me ready for a new run,
Like my journey has just begun.
Being here brings a smile back to my face,
Now that I'm here my dreams I will chase,
Used to be the same shit different day
But now that's not the case,
The pain has finally been erased.
Just like when I saw the California sun,
It has erased all that is done,
Made me ready for what's to come,
My journey has just begun

45

My feet covered in mud,
Mouth full of blood,
Knuckles cut and bruised
From the battles I knew I'd lose
Eyes burning from the lack of sleep
No more tears left to weep
Somehow the pain still seeps
Deep in my heart it still creeps
The red stained my hands
From burying you in the sand
That's what you get, when you fuck me
anyway you can
Ears still ringing from the loud pop
That came from the gun shot
It's you, I more or less forgot.

Hollow black eyes

She took my damn life,
Her fake words cut like a knife
Wish I would have known she wasn't right
That her heart was dark as night
Her devil had already taken flight
Her deadly grip was hard to fight
The most poisonous bite
That turned my happiness to depression at
midnight
By no means were her intentions alright
Her words forever impolite
I saw everything but the light
Trying not to hurt myself, but I just might

Sarcastically... I love you

I love your one way streets,
Your standards I do not meet,
How you always make me take the back seat,
That you feed my jealousy.
I love how you keep me warming the bench,
How you're such a wench,
That you cannot choose a side of the fence,
How your words never make sense.
I love how I always have to play tug of war with the
boys,
That you never given me the choice,
That you drown out the sound of my voice,
How you play me like a toy.
I love that you can never look me in the eyes,
How you hide what you feel inside,
How you act like everything is alright,
How tired I get of the lies.
I love that you're a bitch,
That you hurt me like a stitch,
How you forget me like it's a cinch,
When I cave with a twinge
I love how I try so hard for one chance,
That everyone else gets one with just a glance,
That you have more than enough to romance,
I just cannot snap out of this trance
I love when you roll your eyes,
That you don't care that I've thrown myself at you
more than enough times
That you never make me feel worthy of your time,
with those long sighs,
How comfy you look sitting behind my enemy lines.
I love how you always replace me with someone else
That you make me want to hurt myself
How you lied about everything you felt
That I cannot stand it, that you still make my heart
melt
I love how I'm never your one,
How you keep me sprung,

How you force me to bite my tongue,
That I love you so much, I never want you
gone.
But most of all,
I love that you don't catch me when I fall,
You push me aside after all,
Leaving me to die, against your stone cold
wall.

Finally

The first time alone with you
Such a feeling of happiness like I never knew
I tried not to stare at the beauty that was before me
But you were all I could see
It felt like I've waited forever for that moment
That night with you was sweeter than a glazed
doughnut
I remember the 1st time I laid eyes on that
gorgeous face
You made this heart of mine race
You were that heavenly figure I called my
saving grace
I wanted so badly for you to be the queen to
my ace
I have that chance now to make you mine
I will love you till the end of time
Hold you close as our hearts combine
Every day with you is like dancing in the warm
sunshine
It's like waking up from that magnificent
happy dream
And you didn't want it to end, makes you want
to scream
Till she kisses you, as her eyes gleam
She fills your heart with happiness and
warmth like a hot sun beam
Finally my reality of heaven is lying right next to me
And there is nowhere I'd rather be
She loves me so much and this I see
My baby, she loves thee

My prayer

I do not have the will to fight,
I've used all my dying might
I cannot go on one more sleepless night
I am sorry for this, but it feels right
Happiness is so far from my sight
The devil has taken too many bites
I want to run as fast as I can to the light
In hopes that your arms will hold me tight
Never look at me in fright
I promise it will be alright
Just give me a long kiss goodnight
Until I parish at midnight
The black will forever be my Christ.

My Valentine

This lil' poem I wrote to you from my heart
I love you more each day, than I did from the start
You're so good to me, my sweetheart
The love we share is so beautiful, like art
Your passionate kisses put me in a trance
Looking deep into your eyes, my heart does the happy
dance
The way the light glistens off your beautiful eyes
Girl you have me so mesmerized
The sweet scent of your soft warm skin
Tells me I finally found my heaven
I love that I can always make you laugh
Baby you are totally rad
You're so special you take away the bad
I love you with all the love I have
That joyous smile makes my day
I want to be your forever, I'm not afraid
If you were all mine you have my guarantee
I would devote my all to making you happy
So if you will be my honey bee
I will forever be your honey

A house far from home

Right here, is where I've taken all I can take
When my fists uncontrollably shake
I knew I had made a mistake
I feel the inside of me start to break
You said there would be change
But things remained the same
I thought maybe it was a phase
But to this it quickly came
You act different when others are around
Making it sound like I'm the fucking clown
When it's just us, that's when your words,
slam me to the ground
How far you are capable of bringing me down
If they only knew, you're the dirty hound
Slammin' back that aluminum
Anything to keep you fucking numb
 Thinking you're really foolin' em
But you're just plain dumb
I just do not understand
Why our love is never on the mend
Every time you carelessly lend your hand
You lead me to a dead end
So this is where I no longer give a damn
My respect for you has too much bend
We are too far gone to make amends
So I'm gone, my love I'll send.
As our silence confirms
There is no point of return
As these tables start to turn
The sooner you're gonna learn
We cannot resurrect what has been burned
So I stand on my decision, completely firm
This anger builds with velocity
Towards each other is so much animosity
 So heartrending are your atrocities
I stay silent, as it peaks your curiosity
I'm angrier with you now, than I was back then
Fed up with all your contradictions
Weary of the constant dissensions

I'm scared by your afflictions
As you hide behind your addiction
 It just creates more tension
You just want that fucking attention
And you wonder why I don't listen
You just won't let go
It feels like I'm in a damn choke hold
This distance so it grows
And my feelings keep getting cold
How many times does it need to be told?
So much anguish has destroyed this household
From years and years ago
All we have now, is countless woes
As the plaster on these walls
Hide the matters of the unsolved
In this life I will continue to evolve
Because you chose to dissolve

Heartthrob

You're my blushing beauty, damn so fine
Making you happy is a goal of mine
In my head, I'm always with you passing time
So let me tell you, what's on my mind
Hey, my pretty lady
You should be my steady
My one and only baby
Just do not say maybe
You have the killer 3
Smart, sassy, and sexy
Girl, them thighs
Get me so hypnotized
Along with those mesmerizing eyes
So gorgeous, no one can deny
I picture you in that teddy
That's when I get sweaty
My heart beats with intensity
Girl, we would be a perfect melody
I swear, we have that chemistry
Listen, those legs are driven me crazy
Then everything but you gets hazy
I want to lay you in a bed of daisies
No way would I be hasty
Take off those silk panties
Your lips, I bet taste like candy
We should get hot and heavy
I'll be the mashed taters to your gravy
To have you in actuality
Would be a beautiful reality
You standing before me
Hella better than any fantasy
When I see you on my TV
This is what I see
I see this beautiful babe lying on the sand
Soakin' up the sun getting on your tan
As you slide down those ray bans
Baby girl I'm your #1 fan
Taking ahold of my hands
I spin you around and you're laughin'

Loving you every way I possibly can
Enjoying you being my woman
Your entire body I would osculate
My life to you, I would consecrate
Deep and true my words I would articulate
All night with you, I would copulate
Baby I know it's me you never knew
But damn those baby blues
I want to show you something new
Like how my words soothe
As I whisper I love you
Girl, just be my boo boo
With me there is no heart achin'
Just the feeling of being so awakened
Those perfect pink lips are so captivatin'
Along with your kittenish smile that's breathtakin'
I would do silly things to make you grin
Like kiss that adorable dimple in your chin
I bet the scent of your skin
Oh that vanilla, would draw me right in
I'm saying, I don't care where you have been
Since a you without me is a sin
My heart beats like the bass from a Bose
Just like when I bust your music on my stereo
For years, I've watched you unfold
Like petals from a blooming spring rose
How well you wear repose
Make beautiful art out of your lows
Still look classy with a pierced nose
You wear it best, in casual clothes
The way your hair sweeps across your face
How foxy you look in that lace
Your presence is always with grace
I just want to hold you in my embrace
I know you would appreciate the little things
Like bringing you bubble gum flavored ice cream
Anything to keep that alluring mouth smiling
For you babe, I'd do anything
In that Cali breeze
You sitting next to me

With you is where I want to be
I'll be everything you need
We going to make history
You know it girl, legendary
I'll take you higher than all the trees
Our love will be deeper than all the seas
Baby you're my heartthrob
You got my head gone like oh my gawd
I smile when you talk
I see your beautiful face, my stomach drops
As the sun glistens in your eyes
They light up this cats' dark skies
You are such a cutie pie
Anything you ask of me, I would happily
comply
The most divine woman I have ever seen
Your skin looks so soft and sheen
The contours of your face, are designed so
clean
If my life were a kingdom, you would be the
queen
You surpass my heavenly dreams
I wait patiently for the day we can convene
You are the perfect sunset picture
Each moment with you, would get richer
Through time, the bond between us would get
thicker
We would be the perfect mixture
As we sail together on this adventure
I swear, I'll always say your name like a
scripture

Enrage

There is a rage inside of me that will not sleep
When I find you, its venom suddenly seeps
Inside of me by the heaps
It settles in so damn deep
It has set a fire to my veins
A flood of unconscious to my brain
Puts my emotions in chains
Oh shit, here comes the train
Momentum is what this anguish gains
It's something my heart cannot sustain
As the knots in my stomach start to twist
Indentations on my palms from clenching my fists
Scars left deep in my wrists
From failures I made to you to exist
Mouth filled with blood from eating my tongue
Air so cold around me I feel it in my lungs
I've turned into something so numb
Waiting anxiously for the angel to hum
But my iced embrace has frozen her wings
It's the devil I swear making me do these things
If I could just hear her softly sing
I know the pain would stop lingering
Hatred makes my eyes burn red
From constant tears that I shed
Watching you and all the others tread
I'd rather watch you burn instead
My ears are ringing and hot to the touch
I let the dark get the best of me too much
The hurtful things I've seen, I've had enough
You're just a nonesuch
It has pulled my angry trigger
I thought it was jealousy, but it's something much
bigger
Like all the times I've been put through the ringer
My heart on a silver platter I deliver
You are so disgusting
I want to destroy your something
Till I feel absolutely nothing

Again, I feel this anger coming

Karma is coming

Remember karma is a bitch,
She will make you twitch,
I will not be holding my hand out
Especially when you shout
Nobody will help an evil queen
Especially one that plots deadly schemes
You think you're slick
 I smell your shit
You cannot out smart this lasting pawn
I've figured you out far beyond
It's time for you to pay for all your wrongs
When you're lying in pain on the floor
 Karma isn't done with you,
She's coming back for more

Eye

The thought of being in love again, is scarier than rotting in hell,
Sitting here in the coldest, most dark cell.
Wishing for just one ray of sunlight from and angel,
Come and save me lil' precious one, I know you'll make me well.
Head is spinning out of control, I cannot stop this feeling
Death is something that is highly deeming,
Anything life destructive is very appealing,
Nothing seems to start this healing,
I need the devils poison to keep me awake,
She will not let me stop dreaming of her face,
Cannot get it together long enough, I feel so astray,
Letting myself sink this low was a big mistake,
Addicted to this pain like it's dope
Hanging at the end of my rope,
If I let go now, I'll no longer have to cope,
With this painful demon that has awoke,
As I lie withering away, I see the cloak,
Walking slowly towards me as I start to choke.
As she kneels down before me and removes her hood,
I've finally came to realize something I never understood,
She was the reason I wanted to die,
Smothering me and not letting me far from her side,
I feel the cold fill me inside
She finally gave me wings so I could fly.

HeavenLee

Her eyes made my mouth water, so chocolatey sweet
All the other candies I gazed upon became obsolete
Such softness behind the brown
My at ease feeling was so profound
Insatiable was her kiss
Intoxicating was her spit
Her mouth tasted like winter mint
Soft as rose petals were her lips
Luscious C cup tits
I couldn't keep my hands off it
I clenched onto her strong hips
She passionately touched my face
I couldn't get enough of her minty taste
Her skin smelled of the naked bees
She definitely got this face to cheese
Her soft warm hands on my face
Reminds me of the hot summer days
I put my fingers through her long silky hair
Into my eyes she would stare
Life isn't so dark with you around
Years ago, it's you, I wish I had found.

Painfully obvious
I love you when you roll your eyes,
Your "I don't care" you can't disguise
So hypocritical you should realize,
You're not one to criticize,
People believe your deceitful lies,
You cannot hide from my painful cries,
I know how dark you are inside,
About as dark as your damn hair dye.

Savior

All those times I thought I hit hard when I fell,
I never touched the ground, you caught me I could
tell
Kept pushing me on and gave me the will
Reminding me that you are here for me still
I know it was your decision to make
Your own road to your fate
But if I could go back in time, the gun I would take
Hold you tight and tell you I can relate.
Together we will make it through the hate
You held my hand when all I could see
was dark sights
Made me feel more than alright
Filled my heart back up with love by the pints
Kept life flowing through the hard
wiring in my chests
Made me strive for my success
Wish I could have done the same for you
Hold out my arms pushing you through
Squeezing the trigger you wouldn't
think to do
Now all I can think is, god damn I miss you
When the sun shines warm on my face
I know it's your loving embrace
Even though you are invisible to my eyes
I send a kiss to the skies
I know that's where you reside
You're standing tall by my side
My precious guardian you are keeping me alive
When I want to give up you whisper just drive
Do not ever look behind
Never push your life into rewind.

Dedicated to: Weeny

Obliterate

It's not me, so it must be you
The need for someone new
Must have been way over due
If you only knew
I was fine before you
So I'll be fine when we are through
I'm glad you are out of my life
Made room for Mrs. Right
I'm your loss
I took your shit like a boss
Our memories will be your cost
It's me, you forever lost
Making me feel like I fell short
You should have practiced more at this
purport
Later on you will feel remorse
When you want me back after your divorce
There is no place for me here
You have made that painfully clear
So go get yourself a beer
As I drowned myself in tears
Seemed like you were in it for the long haul
You ignored me for his phone calls
My damn heart you continued to maul
Squeezing the back of my neck, forcing me to
crawl
I felt you slipping from me
I felt the difference in your sincerity
But you swore I was out of touch with reality
Of the situation in its totality
Saying you needed your space
No tears fell from your face
Suddenly I felt so misplaced
I knew then I was replaced
I wish your smile I could efface
Stop placing the blame on me for the debase
These memories, I refuse to constantly retrace

How comfortable you look in someone else's
embrace
I bet it's lies you spew
When you are asked of me and you
Saying I'm the one that found someone new
But we both know that shit isn't true
You're the one fucking another dude
In fact now it's two

Rock to my roll

You're the rock to my roll
Baby anywhere you want go
I will definitely follow
Being with you I'm never low
Only good times
Like I'm dancing in the sunshine
You keep me so happy inside
This feeling is so divine
Just want to make you mine
I swear you will always be satisfied
You make my heart beat a fast pace
Every time I see your beautiful face
All day I just can't wait
Your dreamy lips I want to taste
Holding you, looking into your eyes I melt
These little jolts of happiness I felt
No words to describe
These feelings I feel inside
But I will try my best
I'm in love with you, I confess
You can feel it when your head is on my chest
This love I will express
You're my everything
For you I would do anything
Happiness forever to you I'd bring
A future of us is so promising
I found serenity in your eyes
And rest finally in my nights

The silence
I hate that I cannot get my mind to pass by
That devious look in your eyes
Every time you gave me a careless goodbye
That made me want to die
Your too selfish to hear my silent cries
You wear kindness as your disguise
But I know the truth behind your lies
All your fools cannot see through the blind
You pushed me to want my demise
But through your bullshit I've grown wise
And for this I will rise.
So I hope you're gripping that pillow tight
Better yet, I have something for you to cuddle with right here,
It has a fast trigger, and a hot barrel pointing at your ear.

Drifted

Pain, is the only word I'm thinkin'
When these thoughts come a creepin'
Into my mind
My heart is sinkin'
And butterflies are eaten
By your selfish lies
Did you even think twice?
About your mindless vice
Now my heart pays the price
Of the aftermath from your heart of ice
I loved you endlessly, but still I did not suffice
Angry, is this overwhelming feeling
I feel when I'm not healing
Because you swore I'd get a fair try
He must have been more appealing
Or his heart was worth stealing
Do not tell me lies
The empty look inside your eyes
Girl you cannot deny
His jokes get you high
But his love just gets you by
Did you even think twice?
About your mindless vice
Now my heart pays the price
Of the aftermath from your heart of ice
I loved you endlessly, but still I did not suffice
Relief, I felt this weight lifted
Our memories I've sifted
Realizing you were never worth my time
What you did to me was twisted
Now I have drifted
So I can breathe when you say goodbye.

Happy

As I gaze into your beautiful eyes
I can see this is where my future lies
This feeling I cannot disguise
No one can love you quite like this guy
You give it away when we kiss
That it's me you dearly miss
Things I want in my life, you are at the top of that list
What we have is worth every risk
Granted our situation is tough but we pull through it
Together we are strong and we will make it through this
My beautiful girlfriend for you
There is nothing I wouldn't do
With me you will never be blue
Because we are one, no longer two
Trust me when I say you are the best
You definitely surpass the rest
You're the reason I have a heart beating in my chest
I want you and only you, I deeply express

Back when

Shove me in another locker bitch,
Hit me with your fucking spit,
I know you do not give a shit.
Making fun of how I dress, I'm aware of it,
Sorry my clothes are not as rich as yours,
Not my fault my family was dirt poor,
You think you're all high and mighty
When you pick on ones' like me
Dumping my food on me at lunch,
Oh yeah bitch, you're so tough
Pull my hair again stupid cunt,
What's that? Oh I'm the runt.
Embarrassing me, pulling down my shorts in class,
Laughing and saying you're going to kick my ass.
You can never just pass me by in the hallway
You always have some lame ass shit to say.
Calling me a little queer and I'm such a dike.
If you only knew why my hair was spiked.
I've seen you on the streets now,
You turned your fake ass right around,
What? You're afraid it's you I'm going to clown?
That's right bitch you are on my side of town,
Even too coward to come apologize,
Chicken shit, cannot even look me in the eyes,
Just remember you will get what you deserve,
When life throws you that hard fucking curve

The crush

I watched you from far away
I could never find the words to say
More than just a hi or hey
I regret it nowadays
I would see you every now and then
I'd let you pass me by, time and time again
But to me you have always been
This rush in my heart of adrenaline
I would often fantasize
About those gorgeous eyes
Sitting with you under starry skies
One thing I will never deny
You have always given me butterflies
Not everyone gets to kiss their crush
But the greater things in life shall not be rushed
I've waited forever for one touch
That moment I have longed for, so much
The first time your lips pressed on mine
Was sweeter than dark red wine
The way you held my face
Was intimate with your grace
I will not let you go
Your hands I will hold
As in life, together we will grow
Making this strong bond of love a mold
You're all I'll ever need and want in my life
I hope someday you will become my wife
I love you so much I'd marry you twice
Life with you will be paradise

Through the wicked woods
Could you be my savior?
Save me from my destructive behavior
Could you save me from this hell?
I cannot take any more of this cold cell
Do you feel me when I bleed?
When this rage burns inside of me
Do you guide me when I cannot see?
Shove me when I'm walking aimlessly
Do you push when I'm running to break free?
There is no tread left on my tired feet
Are you there to soothe my nerves?
When life throws these hard curves
Do you clear my mind when it's disturbed?
When therapy doesn't seem like a cure
Will you act as this Adderall?
When I'm bouncing off the damn walls
Will I be that angel that falls?
When the devil calls
These walls are dripping with sin
Are you the one who paints them?
Red eyes all on me from the demons
Did you let them in?
The past has become obsolete
Only when I feel complete
The cuts on the bottoms of my feet
Did you care, you're infected with deceit?
Sweet serenity I continue to seek
Please, do not follow me.

Decisions

Sitting in this airport,
Wondering if it's fair to sell myself short,
If I was smart, I'd walk out them doors,
I know outside, there is so much more
But I have this damn voice
That makes it a hard choice
I know it will take a while to enjoy
No time to be this coy
The time is now
So make them proud.

Loving you

I love you, is so sincere
Why? Because you are my air
Words cannot begin to describe what you mean to me
The one thing that shines bright about you, is your personality
Being with you shows me what love is supposed to be
I just want you to know I want "we"
I will not let anything tear us apart
You will always have this cats heart
I love you so much, It's hard to explain it
There is nothing more in this world I want I happily admit
It's you, only you, and always will be you I mean when I say
You're so special and dear to me in your own unique way
I will not let you pass by
I will not just say goodbye
Till the end, for you I will fight
Till I get to hold you for the rest of my life
And in this moment I again realize
Who needs Paradise?
When with you, every second is a summer sunrise

Counting the flowers

I'm going to make you aware of this,
You're as evil as deaths kiss
Past relationships are a long list
Your face, I want to hit with my fist
Every time I see you, I am totally pissed
You're such an inconsiderate bitch
I sent you roses, but you didn't make anyone aware of it,
Guess I was just your step on
Use me up, till I was all gone
I hate you, yeah far beyond
All these boys you be playin'
All you're wanting is a good layin'
They do not have shit on me
That you could never see
You represent yourself as a whore,
Does your new fad know his time is up when you get bored?
When you're on to your next victim
They will never know what hit them
Ha! You think she is going to change for you
Then you still have a thing or two
That you need to learn about her dude
When you're wallowing in your loneliness counting the hours
You will realize she was using fools like you to collect flowers.

Smack

Rhyme that shit talk,
You can start kicking rocks,
I'm that bass in the boom box,
Makes you do a funny walk,
Like you just got electro shock
You totally piss me off
You act like you're shocked
Chew your words and spit them at your face
Yeah bitch, how does that taste
I'll eat you alive
No way will you survive
Madness in me is what drives
Greatness in me I will strive
I will not let my fire die
Going to expose how I feel inside
When it comes to me
It's like you're getting smacked with a hate
dictionary
I'm definitely out of the ordinary
For you I'm way to extraordinary
Now it's time for you to go
Got you feeling low
How's that feel ho!

Parasite

Her cold slimy lips crept down my neck
As her empty eyes took me back to the train wreck
I felt her frigid presence surround me
The cuts she dug into me so deep
Not even the beautiful angel could stop the bleed
She drank me till I was dry
Leaving no warmth of blood inside
Infected my heart with anguish
Made damn sure it was me she'd vanquish
The painful mind games kept me on my bruised knees
She reminds me anyone's love for her would please
The taste of her sour sweat dripped from my lips
The poison sits silent in her kiss
I'm frozen from the ice in her finger tips
I have never felt so estranged
Setting a fire to my veins
Planting worms in my brain
So forever there she will remain.

My sweet honeybee

There is nowhere I'd rather be,
Than with my beautifully honeybee,
By far better than my dreams
Every second with you becomes more heavenly
There is nothing more I want, than for you to be with
me
I swear I will love you for eternity
So take my hand, and you will see
That we are meant to be
There isn't anyone else I'd rather be with on this
journey
No one else I want to walk beside me.

Coup de Grace

My all to you I gave
Even though your all was fake
At the words I love you, I cave
This was my first mistake
I should have just tied bricks to my legs
And jumped into this fucking lake
To drown these memories I cannot seem to shake
I'm fucking comatose, like I'm twice baked
Sometimes these thoughts are too much to take
Like that time I made you a cake
And you laughed I'm my fucking face
You think this is a game, but it ain't
In the silence, I break
It's you I have to thank
When there is a chance at new love, I hesitate
Stop and reiterate
These puppet strings you yank
My confidence you eviscerate
My mind you adulterate
You've lost your sense on how to commiserate
So my heart you obliterate
That smile you drove me to hate
This perfect artificial picture you paint
Only to give me a teasing taste
I've lost this race
What I thought was love was lust
Our gold turned to rust
Justifying my feelings became a must
So for you I lost the trust
Your lies were so torturous
When I felt it in my gut
That the end was nearing for us
You were slipping away, so the harder I would clutch
How deep your words still cut
Like what the fuck
Seldom a soft touch
Was just enough
To get that rush

Keeping me in love
Then you decide to give up
Now it's gone with a gust
As it scattered us like dust
Now I watch my world crumble like pie crust

Melting into you

Every inch of her body was so tender,
Like a pillow made out of feathers,
Her skin smelled flowery fresh,
The tasted of Ale and mint lingered on her breath
Every kiss was with gentle caress
Listening to her heartbeat as I lie on her chest
My body on hers laced with sweat
We were soak and wet
This feeling was more beautiful than the tropics at
their best
Every bit of her taste so sweet,
I thought I had bitten into a Georgia peach
I wanted to love her head to feet
Her juices dripped from my mouth
The further I went south,
All of her was totally insatiable without a doubt
She held me in her arms,
Her love was so warm,
It shielded me from any harm
My heart would melt in to her hand
She wasn't going to let it turn into sand
Her palms had the power to mend
She kissed my heart and put it back in.

Dear Heart

My heart just popped out of my chest,
Landed on this notebook so I could rest.
When I opened my eyes,
I couldn't believe the sight.
Shattered pieces of her everywhere,
Attempt to put her back together, if I dare.
Each broken piece,
Bled all over the blank paper sheets,
Soaked right through like a fresh piece of
meat.
When I wiped the pages clean,
Something was brought to my attention that
had not been seen.
So many words that were left unsaid.
Were now in my notebook, stained by the red.

Pierced

She is the reason I lost my glow,
 She is dying off and taking my soul,
My heart is screaming no no no,
 Please just let her go,
But it's harder than that ya know,
The writing on this page just goes to show,
She is my undying woe,
 The painful reminder I once loved a ho.
We don't see eye to eye just toe to toe,
 The devil inside her still grows.
Tying my tongue in that bow
 Leaving open the cuts I cannot sew,
Trying to destroy my self- control,
 She keeps me shoveling this heavy ass coal.
She ripped out my soul
 And dropped it into her black hole.

Make you sweat

To me, you're forever in debt,
Since you viciously tangled me in your net
Now I'm going to make you my pet
Let's see how far from your leash you will get
Looks like your shirt is getting a little wet
Faster than a damn turbo jet
Oh that's your boy; I'm going to fucking deck
You think you had your plan set
Till I came along and made you fret
I'm going to make you regret
The first day we met
Nasty ho with hickies all over your neck
I'll fuck your world up that's a threat
Naw better yet
Let's make a bet
That I can make you sweat.

Cold as ice

I was just a check on a bucket list
Thought there was something I missed
But you're just being your normal self, bitch
Wear that shoe, how perfectly it fits
Treated me like a foreclosed home
Fixed me up, then you were gone
Put me up for some else to own
This bullshit, before I wish I had known
Seems now I have become old news
Before, it was me, you could not stand to lose
I sit here with my head in my hands confused
I never would have thought you would leave me so bruised
If I sang through these walls, my blues
Would you still want to live in separate rooms?
Or swear to me our love was doomed
Tell me something to rid this gloom
You're making me so damn emotional
This anger is getting harder to control
I know our situation was dysfunctional
But I was willing to let that go
You washed me away like dirt on a towel
My hand is over my heart like ow!
Everything was so abrupt like wow
I had no idea you would hit me like pow
Lately, your words are less than friendly
Didn't think we would become enemies
But if that's how my heart sees
Then I welcome you to my love hate tragedy

Paradise getaway

Sitting on my passenger side
Enjoying every mile of this ride
Love the way you dance and glide
Baby you make me wish you were my bride
The sun glistening of your tan skin
I just cannot stop grinnin'
This is where I want our life to begin
Your heart I'm dedicated to winnin'
Just seeing your closed eyes behind your Dolce's
Makes all the stress go away
It doesn't even feel like a Monday
Just us and a sunny day
Too cute how you sing every song
I have you to myself I cannot go wrong
With me is where you belong
This day I wish I could prolong
Your arm up on the head rest
My hand on your stomach with gentle caress
Slide down your shade to look at me is the best
You can hear my heart beating outta my chest
Your cutie toes wiggling on your bare feet
Tappin' to the songs beat
I get a whiff of your perfume it's so sweet
You make me feel so complete
Your soft hair done up in curls
Being my lil' country girl
I want to give us a paradise in this crazy world
So baby trust me, let's give us a whirl

Sick of You

I lie here quietly
Trying to rid this anxiety
But the volume goes up on the TV
Why must you always aggravate me
I'm getting addicted to these fucking sleep aides
Because it helps with this undying rage
Your politeness is so staged
Wait till that one fine day
They all find out you're fake
All these things left unsaid
 I let boil over in my head
Oh man here I go again
Bleeding my heart through this pen
Stop acting like you are 5
You have me staring down this gun at my side
The shit I see from the corner of my eye
Bitch, you must want me to die
You smother me like I'm in a plastic bag
Along with a dirty sock for a gag
This love is like a material snag
So easy to unravel, that's a drag
One minute you hate me the next we're cool
Your bipolar ass is fucking coo coo
Remember, I'm no damn fool
I know your amping up for the next duel
Like angels and demons we would feud
You need to fix that attitude
For you force me to have this fortitude
Hate will be with you through your decrepitude
Who's right, who's wrong is long disputed
My past mistakes are so easily mooted
Because in bitch you're so fluent
Our issues are so deep rooted
This anguish cannot be eluted
Sadistic is a word so suited
When my side is totally muted
Taking credit for shit I do
Just ask my sis who she looks up to

I bet my checks it isn't you
Never would you own that one, I knew
So I take a step back
To avoid another attack
This common sense you lack
So my heart turns black
I cannot wait for your skeletons to fall out of your closet
Say I told you so to those who bought it
Now it's time to be honest
Being someone you're not, you're no novice
When our debris settles from the flames
The silence follows like sun after the rain
Your moods change like the wind it's insane
My good side once again you try to gain
I've told you before you need help
But you cannot admit it to yourself
Save your hugs and kisses for someone else
Cuz these sticks and stones, at me, you continually pelt
Words from your mouth will keep me sore
While you're busy keeping the score
The tenderness of I love you is nevermore
These feelings I cannot feel anymore.

Sweet sunrise
I caught the sunrise,
As it was passing me by,
Helped me cut the ties,
Forget the lies,
Release the deep sighs,
Dried my eyes,
Killed the madness inside,
Silenced the cries,
Found happiness in the skies,
Only put anger where it applies,
Didn't let regrets pry,
Helped with the goodbyes,
Made me more wise,
Convinced me it was going to be alright,
Tucks me in at night,
Forever I can now sleep tight,
So when I open my eyes,
Next to me would lie,
My sweet sunrise.

Banished Love

I do not love you anymore
You wanted me, I could have swore
Your tireless routine is such a bore
So nasty you are, whore
Being with you was a fucking chore
It was once you I adored
From the start, I should have believed the
folklore
No longer are you my Amor
This is rest assured
I'm cutting this cord
Not one damn tear was shed
As you destroyed everything I am
You wanted some chump instead
Inside, my love for you is dead
Not a flinch as you kicked me out
I knew exactly what it was about
Wasn't because you had "too much" going on
You used me up, now you wanted me gone
Played me like a fucking pawn
Till someone funnier came along
Left me like damn, floored
My words were rudely ignored
Texting while my heart, out I poured
It's cool, I don't want to interrupt, I'll show
myself the door

Daddy

Liar is your name,
Cheating is your game.
Always the drink to blame,
You're such a damn shame.
Too busy with your women,
Blew our money on lucks driven winnins'
When I was young I would hang on your leg
"Don't go to the bar" I would desperately beg
To those who were dear
Would never compare to your beer.
Anything to drown your little girls' tears.
Promises you would never keep,
I would lie in my bed countless times and weep
While you're out playing your game of deceit
Memories of us should be fond,
But it's hard to have any, when you were always gone
You let that go on for too long
Once in a while I'd get you to myself,
You're still bitter about the hand you were dealt
Any chance you could get you would ditch
Because you'd rather be with your bitch
You're missing out on your little girls' growing up
It's cool, I got it I'll teach my lil sis all the fatherly
stuff
It's your loss you missed all those years
Maybe someday when you look back you'll be the
one in tears.

The cats' pajamas

You opened my eyes to clear skies of blue,
An angel sent from above, is what I found in you.
At my weakest breaking point, ready to vanish away,
You picked me up and gave me a reason to stay.
Thought the pieces of my heart had rotted and burned
to ash,
I quickly realized it still lives and beats hella fast.
Nothing compares to the feeling I get when I see you
smile.
A feeling I thought I had lost, it was gone for a while.
The sound of your heartbeat eases my raging
emotions,
What I feel for you goes deep as oceans,
You took my pain and made it into beautiful sunshine
rays,
I just keep hoping you're here to stay.
Wanting to kiss those perfect lips in the most
passionate way,
Never thought I'd miss you throughout the day.
I love you more each and every day,
Making sure our feelings don't go astray.
Your laugh is something I like a lot,
The giggle is so cute, how could I not.
The sexiest laugh lines ever made by a grin,
Sends my built walls tumblin'
You make my days amazingly better,
You're as beautiful as the summer weather.
Your smile leaves me speechless with no words to
say,
When you hold me tight you take my breath away.
You're all I see in a crowded room,
You make my heart go boom boom.
When you put your sexy hands on me,
I cannot help but to think naughty.
Such a jammin' gorgeous body lips, hips, and tits,
Sends my imagination on pure bliss.
The walk of a woman, who will kick your ass,
Turns me on to know you will always have my back.

Damn that bombshell fragrance has me trippin'
You make me laugh no matter what mood I'm in.
I forget where my life has been.
You're definitely the knot to all my loose ends.
You make everything go away, your personality is the
greatest,
Sending all my bad on a long hiatus.
Baby girl, you're so wonderful, you make my heart
go bananas,
Because to me, you are the cats pajamas.

Cut me out

I thought I saw heaven in your eyes
But it was a prison hidden by your lies
Now I see how inauthentic you are
I wish back then, my thoughts of you were smart
I would not have allowed you to tear me apart
Fuck these scars
Fuck you, for it's me, you disregard
And fuck you for eating my heart
Breaking me like it was an art
You're just a monster lurking in the dark
Saying bullshit to give me hope
I keep tying knots in this rawhide rope
Holding a knife to ones' throat
Just so I do not sing you a nice note
Or say to you another loving quote
Take you back the answer is nope
I say that's all this cat wrote
My love for you, you have forced to erode
Your deceptiveness, has clearly shown

Smile

Those gorgeous eyes staring at me
Ever so intensely
I want you so damn immensely
The chocolate color was rich like a Bentley
I get to thinking could this be
Have I found that one?
I'm totally all about you hun
Thoughts that race through my mind of us are so
intense
You and I just make sense
You definitely can solve a stressful day
Just by that adorable smile upon your face.

Why I adore you

I know you don't like the color of your eyes
But baby let me tell you they are as beautiful as a
Caribbean sunrise
I love that we can talk all through the night
And the squeak you make when I pull you in to hold
you tight
These crazy butterflies that with you I get
I smile cutting your chicken up real small I admit
When you can't drink your chocolate milk without
spooning it
Laying and holding you next to me we are a perfect
fit
Shaking your head as I tell you how beautiful you are
Baby I'm for real, I love every inch and every scar
You're certainly my heavenly angel by far
And even though you think you need it, you don't
need Pure Barre
So wonderful inside and out I cannot stop gazing
I know you do not believe me when I say you are
amazing
But I'll show you every day till you get the meaning
Making you my wife is highly deeming
You are so damn beautiful, you say I'm crazy
But in a crowded room you're all I see baby
I love the smile you get when I bring you daisies
Just laying around with you being lazy
So cute how you rock back and forth in the shower
I'm falling for you more and more by the hour
The scent of your skin is like a blooming spring
flower
I cannot stop thinking damn I want to spend my life
with her
You think other girls are prettier than you
But they do not even come close, I wish you knew
Your loving heart is so undeniably true
No one can ever compare to
I cannot just let you pass me by
I'm going to make you all mine

Babe if all you need is a little time
I'm going stay right by your side
I love it when you pull me close when you want me to
stay
And hold my hand to let me know it's ok
I know you think these feelings are going to change
Far down the road when we are old and grey
But none of that matters I'm still going to adore you
anyway
Biggest grin when you're painting the nails on my feet
When I make a funny face and you're laughing at me
When you caress my cheek to kiss me passionately
All these things I love babe, and I want to be your one and
only

The devil herself
Your demons made you with precision,
Your heart is where they made their incision
Being the queen of hell was your decision
You're so diabolical in my vision
It's the devil you do well in your derision
Destroy all innocents is your mission
Your poison is always cooking in hell's kitchen
You feel no emotion not to mention
You definitely have problems
Not even a psychiatrist can solve them
Something is loose in your head
Your evil is spoon fed.

Bullet

One word from her mouth,
Goes through my brain and doesn't find its way out.
I'm at a constant war within myself.
I have to pull the trigger fast there's no doubt.
Her selfishness eats at my mind.
Robs my heart blind,
I hear the chamber click,
As I start to feel sick.
Just rid me of my anguish,
There is too long of a list.
I can no longer find the reason to stay.
I cannot go on one more antagonizing day.
So please just burn through me clean,
I promise they won't hear me scream.

Scene

Maybe I made these words hurt,
Maybe I don't care if I'm a jerk,
I'm just hitting you with what you deserve,
Come back for me again you're going to get served.
With one hell of a hard curve,
I thought by now you would have learned,
You keep fucking with me you will get burned,
I'm like a hot plate,
Touch me, you will get baked.
I'm going to chew you up like gum,
Spit you in the trash when I'm done
Smash you like mashed potatoes
Take you down like a tornado,
Fucking with me is fatal
My words are the vice grip
I'll crack your skull like a nutcracker bitch
You need your "garden" sprayed with a different hose
every night.
Me telling the truth about you make you want to fight
I'm the one you're going to learn to hate
Now let's see what kind of scene you're going to
make

Truth

She says I'm so crazy
I get her back with only bout you baby
The way the light glistens off the brown in your eyes
Makes me melt every time
She gives me that come get it stare
Ravish her body with my love, no one can compare
Make you mine forever yes I do dare
 My life with you I want to share.
I love the way you cross you strong tan legs sitting in
a chair
Standing there wearing just your grey sweater
Girl you get me wetter and wetter
Clenching on to the bones in your hips
I slightly drool kissing your peppermint lips
The passion in your kiss
I know it's me you miss
Your sexy naked body in front of me I will admit
So many naughty things I want to do to it
Gently caressing your supple breasts
Leaving my wet lip prints on your neck
As your silky soft hair grazed my cheek
I knew we would make love perfectly
I love you like the stars love the sky
It's you that has caught my eye
This feeling I cannot deny
I love you truly, no lie.

Uncle

I sat next to your grave,
As a gentle breeze touched my face.
I knew it was your loving embrace,
A chill to me it gave.
I wasn't ready to say goodbye,
But you were ready to fly.
Nevermore you wanted to cry,
I wish at the time,
I was old enough to realize why.
You had so much strife
I could have brought you back to life,
Showed you, life isn't as bad as it seems,
Hugged you tight when I heard your silent
screams.
I know how you felt,
But sometimes a shitty hand is what we are
dealt.
If you were here today,
There is one thing I'd definitely say,
No bitch is worth the bullet,
So fuck her, you will get through it.
I wish I wasn't at the time so young,
Could have given you strength to put down
the gun.
But I also realize why you did it,
You were at the end of your rope and said
fuck this.
You didn't think you could make it through no
more,
Just you had no idea you had so much to live
for.
One day I will get to see you again soon,
But till then, know that I totally miss you.

Dedicated to: Weeny

What was it that you said?

I watched your eyes glaze over as I talked about us,
I knew deep down you did not give a fuck.
Always concerned with your own needs,
But as for mine, you're too blind to see,
I'm breaking down emotionally.
You're busy planning your exit strategy,
You cannot wait till I set you free.
Why do you always come back?
Knowledge of loving someone is what you lack.
You cannot stand when someone hates you,
Grabbing my heart and dragging it back to you.
I don't understand why you choose me,
To keep as your dependency.
You do not even listen to the things I say,
You put your head down or walk away.
You cannot even remember things about me,
You're hung up on the next boy you're going to go see.
I find us at the beginning again,
Trying to get my point across your thick head,
When all I rather do is lie next to you instead,
Then you look up and say "what was it you just said?"

The One

I love you more than anyone would believe
You I will never deceive
When the sun is shining in your eyes looking
at me
The ambient light shines so brightly
Your love knows the right path to take
Hold my hand and guide me in this life we
will make
Make me feel good like I used to feel
Kiss my lips to keep em sealed
You're my rainbow after a dark storm
Being with you, makes me feel reborn
Waking up next to that smile
Makes the pain worth while
Feeling the sense of ease in my mind
The serenity you have put inside
Just one touch and the hairs stand up on my
arms
The lil' things you do, makes this cat charmed
One day we won't have to close our eyes
Make a wish that we are at each other's side
I'm ready to take life with stride
Baby you are my life

This is truth

Making up lies, on why you do not want me
Try being honest with yourself honey
It's cause I do not make all that money
And dress "oh so cunning"
Or have that cock to shove in your face
No lie, I know you like that taste
You are so counterfeit, it's a disgrace
Selfishness, in which it is based
Making people believe your love is so good
But behind closed doors it's misunderstood
He doesn't treat you like he should
You are living a double life in this falsehood
Intrigued? More like infatuation
Your words were such a contradiction
Think you're putting me at ease with the speech on
"separation"
Foolish I was to my own desperation
Only puts on a show for others to see
To trick people into thinking y'all are happy
What a crock of shit
I see right through it
Why waste each other's time
Better yet, why the fuck did you waste mine
Love and hate for me is a thin line
Are you sure you can handle my opine
Oh, I'm the greatest?
Your bullshit is so overrated
Just wanted to play me like a game in Vegas
No opinion just a clear statement
Hope Romeo knows the latest
Yeah bitch, my writing about you, famous

Goodbye

She handed me the gun and said here,
Please do not shed any tears.
I know I hurt you so bad my dear,
So point the barrel at me and set your mind
clear.
I knew what had to be done,
I had control of the gun,
Releasing all her flesh eating demons,
To watch would be fun.
I took one last look in her eyes,
And she took her last deep sigh,
She spoke her last words "you know I always
loved you right?"
I closed my eyes and said goodbye.

E.D.C.

Baby girl you are my E.D.C.
Take my hand and you will see
Our love is easy like 1,2,3
You're better than any fantasy
At the risk of sounding cheesy
Girl you complete me
When we chillin'
It's straight Illin'
Is it your heart I'm stealin'?
Then tell me how you're feelin'
And if it's a broken heart you're concealin'
Then let me be the one to do the healin'
Moonlight gracefully dances on your skin
Sweat on your chest looks like diamonds glistnin'
Your eyes tell me what you want and baby I'm
listenin'
Lips so perfectly sweet, I cannot stop kissing them
Soothing as the waves hitting the shore is your
intimacy
Just one touch, is pure ecstasy
Inhale the sweet scent on your neck
I close my eyes and think this is perfect
Girl you make me sweat
Weak in the knees is what I get
Your hand intertwined with mine
As I scoot you closer to make our bodies combine
I can feel your heartbeat increase
The more I make funnies
This is where I want to be
For eternity just you and me.
Baby girl you are my E.D.C.
Take my hand and you will see
Our love is easy like 1,2,3
You're better than any fantasy
At the risk of sounding cheesy
Girl you complete me
Even though you think I tell all the ladies this
You're the only one that I see myself being a family

with
I run my fingers through your long silky hair
Giving me that heavy loving stare
I can tell, that for me, how deeply you care
I love all the little silly things we share
Because babe, you make this cat, smile shine
Especially when I feel our hearts combine
The day that you say to me I do
Would be like a dream come true
Kissing those soft flower petal lips
Touching your beautiful body with my fingertips
I just cannot get enough of it
Our time together is so precious
Your love is as gentle as a summer breeze
Your beauty is more beautiful, than the colors in
autumn leaves
I am thankful for the great lengths you go to please
The glistening in your eyes, those moments, I wish I
could freeze
Because baby you are my E.D.C.
Take my hand, it's you I will never leave
Our love is deeper than any sea
Babe, you are so the bees' knees
The words I speak cannot compare to how I feel
When you look in my eyes my heart suddenly heals
You walked with a heavenly grace into my life
Taking the darkness out of my sight
My vision of the perfect love
It comes from somewhere beyond the stars above
It keeps my feet planted on the ground
With an untouchable feeling that surrounds
So sweet like a first sip of fall wine
A love that can be read right between the lines.
No confusion just easy love
Flying free like the turtle doves
Baby girl you are my E.D.C.
Take my hand and you will see
Our love is easy like 1,2,3
You're better than any fantasy
At the risk of sounding cheesy

Girl you complete me

Take a bow clown

I couldn't see that your love was staged,
So I tried my hardest but my mind became
hazed
I kept falling for you but your storms kept
their rage
Leaving me empty and so fucking dazed
Promises of feelings that you will never show
An undying love that will never grow
You left me far beyond six feet below
You were more beautiful than a red rose grove
Insanity into my head you drove
Your heart is now what I loathe
Our friendship saw fire and dove
Fuck you for giving me these woes
Made yourself my foe
Now you're just a silly ho.

Sweet Honesty

After all the disappointments I never wanted an
apology
I was to focused on our possibilities,
I just wanted you to again love me,
I kept searching for a key
That was going to set free,
This depressing rut of misery
Wanting the closeness of us constantly
The never ending yearning to touch your body
But the destructive patterns that came to be
Made clear the fact you didn't want we
It wiped the dirt from my eyes so I could see,
The person you became was ever so clearly,
You will forever be my sweet honesty.

Trip on me

The pain will drive you insane,
When I resent you and love you in vein.
Your words and affections are so vague,
It feels like all I do is beg.
Locked in your own selfish ambiance,
You're so pretentious you'll be itching for a glance.
All your bullshit is evasive,
But the chaos you bring makes me want to chase it.
When you tell me you love me you prevail,
Then you rip my heart to pieces that you freely avail.
I just couldn't care less,
At least I tried my best.
Since you need you "space",
You're going to let love go to waste.
I will not play your games,
You move your mouth but all the words sound the same.
You've made me feel like I'm desperate,
Now days just a bit reckless.
I thought you were the one,
You let too much poison come undone.
Pushing me away because the game is through,
You do me so wrong yet I'm still crazy for you.
From you, I only get bits and pieces,
You always play me, what the fuck is the reason.
I know my love for you can last for years,
But can my respect last through the tears.
Since love for you is no longer a necessity,
You'll want it back when you run out of your vanity.
So I force this smile,
I know the misery is going to stay awhile.

You used to spend all your time with me,
Now nowhere near me, is where you want to be.
Love is a feeling you'll never choose to use,
Always making up some lame ass excuse.
For loving a mind so sick,
I have to ask, am I masochist?
You're the one with the issues
At least I admit I miss you.
You pushing me far away was your choice,
I hope you're haunted by the pain in my voice.
I will make you eat your words
Your shit is so obscured.
You and your sweet conceit,
Why you always want to trip on me.
Down the road you will be with me if you decide,
Maybe I'll forgive you and maybe you'll finally try.

The L I adore

Her angelic wings embraced me
I laid my head on her shoulder
She whispered I will not leave
It lifted the huge boulder
She was all I would ever need
I'll love you eternally I told her
The light in her eyes I could see
I met my heaven that's for sure
With her I endlessly wanted to be
She is my cure
Her love was the key
That I had been searching for
To set me free
It is her that I adore
The happiness she gives me I did not foresee
I'm in love with her forevermore

Homesick

I miss the smell of when I first walk in
The warmth that surrounded me was so welcomin'
The way the sun shines in as its settin'
How beautiful the décor was within
How easy it was to forget where my life has been
What I would give, to feel like that again
To find where I belong
Thought it was in front of me all along
I believed things were great
Abruptly I was forced away
My all, my everything, I gave
I do not understand why I couldn't stay
Something I did? I cannot say
Only truth I know, I feel so astray
The unknown to the reasons why, on me they weigh
I never wanted to cause such dismay
My home is only where I want to lay
I love my home more than anything, I portray
I tried to open the door, it was locked
I still love my home even after it made my heart stop
I wish I could feel the comfort once more
If only my home would unlock the door
I promise to be better this time
I've made changes in this mind
Even though the last time I was here, it was more than
unkind
I guarantee to bring back the shine
No other place makes me feel like this
It's true, home is where the heart is.

Real deal

Shut the fuck up before I choke you with that
chicken
The only thing your mouth is good for is to
slip a dick in.
The sight of you will forever keep me itchin'
I know you are not that finger lickin'
You need to grow up and quit your bitchin'
Always over nothing, straight trippin'
I will pull this car over and send your ass
hitchin'
Rude? No I'm just the raw deal
I am not afraid to tell you how I feel
Your attention lime light I will steal
Oh yeah bitch I'm so for real.

Wanna be corporate clown
Spineless bastard you definitely are,
Biggest snake by far.
Following big shots around like a little puppy,
You say "oh yea fuck me"
Those guards look like they fit perfect on your knees,
The first to say pick me pick me!
We all see through you so clearly,
You will step on everyone to get to the top,
The best at sucking cock,
Two faced bitch,
You little fucking snitch.
Better watch your back,
You are about to get bitch slapped.
Your head is so far up their ass
When you talk it's like an extra-large shit-mac
We can't even understand you when you speak,
At least take the cock out of your mouth first please.
You're not from this country
Trying to run us into the ground,
I'd like to see you do what we do clown,
Fucking kiss ass you think you're better than
everybody,
When in actuality, you're a nobody
Just remember you're a piss on like us
For yourself you also make it tough
They just using you as their pet
You looking kind of sick now, need a vet?
You're a stupid fucking fool
Around here you are the tool
Ignorant chauvinist trying to disrespect me that isn't
cool
Don't worry you got it coming I got something for
you.
Looking like you jumped out of a Mario game
I'm not the princess I'll make you hang your head in
shame
Your bullshit is so lame
Your "award" just indicates you swallow the most
jizz

Your nose is always in everyone's biz
I'll burn you till you fizz
It isn't my fault your wife cheated and left you
You're a fucking ignorant boy anyone would
dude
I broke the frame to your perfect fucking
picture
How's it feel to have the script flipped and I
ripped ya
You have no idea what it is to be a working
class man
For one you have to actually dirty up your
hands
And two, you sure the fuck aren't a man
You're a lil attention deprived boy who's a
coward
Having others fight your battles that's just
absurd
I'm definitely going to make being around me
awkward
If you like having your face in one piece
I suggest you shut the fuck up before it meets
the concrete.

The realization of her darkness

The sky behind her turned to black,
I knew from here, there was no turning back.
I felt an overwhelming sadness from her grace,
As her arms clenched me in her dark embrace.
I knew what I had to do to escape,
I could no longer make her my fate.
If I were to die, she would not care anyways
Every time it speaks it clogs my airways,
There is a tight rope around my stomach,
Every time you tug me your way, I feel like I want to
vomit
Being with you makes me need a therapist,
I feel like my bolts are loose and shit
You're so damn malevolent
My love for you was always irrelevant
Your mind is playing the role of Hell's kitchen
Your foolish actions keep my eyes dripping
Your dark shadows still lingers behind good people
Dealing them something lethal
If there was ever a time I wanted to hurt you it is now
The killer inside me is profound
Your physical beauty drives me insane
But your inside is what causes me so much pain
All the tears I cried for you,
There isn't enough tissue,
Those demons prey heavily on your back
As you plan your next attack,
But no matter how many bites you take out of my
heart
I will always find a way to make the blood gushing
wounds into art.

Just let you go...

Look in my eyes and see the nothingness in
thee,
You have put this numbness and pain inside of
me.
Know changing your mind to love me now,
Won't change how I feel, I have moved on
somehow.
It sickens me to see the way you treat people
who care,
It's like we do not exist, like we are not even
there.
Didn't anyone ever tell you?
Never break the heart that truly loves you.
Find the happiness you have put in me,
And make it my undying misery.
Putting it out there for everyone else to see.
How difficult you're making my life to be.
You're evil, you have cruel intentions,
I wish my heart had some kind of rejection.
It was never my plan to break,
I want to spit it all back in your face.
You said I was great, so why did you always
want better?
Guess I should have listened when they said
you're a real "go get her"
Now I must leave and be gone,
I've realized you were just keeping me
hanging on.
I'm giving away what I'm feeling for you,
Giving it to someone new,
Someone who deserves me and all that I do.
The hurt you will feel will be too hard to
ignore,
When my world doesn't revolve around you
anymore.
Do not touch me, I cannot stand how you feel,
I'm sorry but I will not make the devil a deal.
I see who you truly are,
I will have to live with this scar.

I am not your toy,
I refuse to fill your voids.
No need to apologize I don't fucking care anymore,
I know you cannot change a whore.
Your dark love will wither away
I will once again be ok.

Vision

A million I love yous', could never compare
To the depth of how deeply for you I care
You're the sand to my ocean
Your love drives my devotion
The way you give yourself to me
There is no pain and my heart is free
Everyone else is just a face
Baby you are my Ace
You make this heartbeat of mine increase in pace
Like I just ran a 100 mile race
I'm counting the seconds in which I can see you next
And I'm always anxiously awaiting your text
You should see this silly smile I get
You would think I'm so cute I bet
I adore the shit outta you
Having you by my side I want to start this life anew
You make me a positive person
You are the one and this I am certain
As we lye here, your head on my chest
This feeling is so soothing it's the best
I want this for the rest of my lifetime
My beautiful angel, say you'll forever be mine.

Shit

That moment I realize
All your words were lies
Right down to loving your eyes
Who knew we would come to demise
Now I'm back to sleepless nights
Someone please tell me why
Does a true love make me cry?
All your actions make me want to die
I thought you wanted to end up with me
But that was all make believe
I feel the distance between us
Gapping larger, losing the trust
I tried so hard, why you must
Take it all away for some damn stray, I'm fucking
bust
Could we walk back to the beginning?
So I could walk away from you, no kidding
These memories have these blues stinging
What do I do now? You forgot me so quick
Like you just chewed me up and spit
Are you sure you don't want to also take a piss
While I lay here fucking sick
I never thought I'd write about you like this
Your way is fucking bullshit

The annihilation
In 14 days her love expires
Nothing seems to quench her desire
She says she still loves me, she is a fucking
liar
The need of her in my life is no longer dyer
Her selfishness I do not admire
Her games, I've grown tired
Tolerance to her bullshit I've acquired
Always looking for the drug to take her higher
But she is the mouse and I'm the jaguar
Just start calling me the annihilator
I know she is a faker
She is never the giver always the taker
I'm going to help her meet her maker
Because I totally hate her.

February (2/18/2007)

Looking so sexy in your tight jeans and band t-shirt,
My eyes never felt so alert,
My words I'm trying not to blurt,
So cute how you flirt.
Didn't waste no time,
Finding me on line,
Talking to me all night,
It just felt so right.
That night we met in February,
Was so sweet like a chocolate Cadbury,
The way your eyes lit up,
Whenever I'd show up.
Biggest grin to greet me,
You couldn't wait to see me.
The way you looked at me,
You were in love deeply.
I was hoping this feeling, was going to last forever
We were going to make it through all the weather,
How soft you kissed my neck,
I had to pinch myself just to check,
Chillin' on my bed when we had the first kiss,
The way you tasted put me in bliss
You were too good to be true,
I knew I would lose you.
Going for long walks,
Our eyes would lock,
Lying next to you was heaven,
Asking myself where you have been,
Your hugs were so warm and loving,
I knew I was your little doveling
When you first held my hand,
I knew our love had began
There was nowhere else I wanted to be,
Then for you to spend your life with me.

Stone

You have that heart of stone,
Doesn't even break when love is thrown
I would have gave up everything I own
For us to have some time alone
It's my heart you have stolen
But you have clearly shown
You will give yours to no one
The way you played me is mind blowin'
My hypothalamus is swollen
For your childish bullshit I'm to grown
I will not be a slave kneeling at your throne
All these lessons about you, I wish I'd already
known
For the future, I'm cautious not to sink with a
stone.

Yours to keep

I'm yours to keep
My love for you no one can beat
You give me chills from my head to my feet
I'll love you forever and that I'll help you see
To you I'll always be true
I'll show you love like you never knew
I'm stuck to you like glue
My life I want to live with you
I love you so much
I just can't wait for one touch
There is just something about the way
The soft breeze swept your hair across your face
As the hot sun kissed your skin
The way my love was sinking in
The sweet scent that passed by my nose
You smile and the faster my heartbeat goes
Overjoyed with happiness is what I'm gettin'
Standing here with you is heaven

The drop

I'm unsure of how this all came to be,
When I started to express the feelings within
me,
I'm sure it had a lot to do with,
All my life's bullshit
Somewhere along its path
I came across a very anguished wrath
It caused my mind to derail
And burst into flames with no avail
I started to hurt more than I can ever imagine
Evil people took their advantage
They let me bleed without handing me a
bandage
My heart, no one could salvage
I was a slave to my own pain
My only friend was the ice cold rain
I let painful things drive me insane
As hate filled my veins
The disturbing thoughts infected my brain.
I have no one but myself to blame
I've tried my best to make good,
Of all depressing situations that left me
misunderstood,
Being the best person I can be like I should.
I never want to live my life in rewind
I never again want to be in that tough bind
Like the first time I fell in love,
I hung my head and noticed the drop of blood.

Depression

You thought you could ignore me and I'd go away?
That's when misery laughed in my face
I'm buried deep in your mind, this is where I'll stay
Good luck convincing them you're not cray zay
The loneliness is soiled in agony
The thoughts are driven by insanity
While hell awaits patiently for me
As I curse silently in blasphemy
I cannot escape this reality
Of depression in its totality
I keep thinking of a way to make a casualty
So it will look like it was done naturally
There are many who love me
But I still feel unhappy
I don't understand why
I have feelings that make me cry
Is this desolation destroying who I am?
And why do I not give a damn
I know I'm a good person
But how I feel still worsens
I thought if I ignored it
It would disappear, I admit
But I cannot hide the truth
I still here my demons clawing my roof
Sooner or later they will get back in
And I'll be too far gone for myself to defend

Thinking straight

Fuck all your mental abuse,
I'm going to hang your bitch ass with my noose
I'll throw my words at you like a dodge ball,
Have you pinned up against the wall
Better watch your back,
I will leave a huge gash
I'll knock you out cold black,
Your eyes are about to meet the facts
You're the best at neglect,
I hope you take time to reflect
How much you affect,
How bad you infect,
You're leaving me a wreck.
So I think its best you go,
This time don't make it slow mo.
I'll try not to let it show,
That I'm finally ready to let you go.
You do not love me anymore,
I will not fall for your allure.

That Feeling

That warm feeling of happiness that tingles through
my veins
The absence of life's pains
How much love I know by being with you I gain
The positivity that is soaked into my brain
How fast my heart beats
Every time our eyes meet
No one can ever defeat
I have found that you hold the key
When I think of years ahead
It's you and only you lying next to me in bed
Your head on my chest as I pet your head
Being grateful for the life to which I was led
And you loving every word I ever said
I found my someone who I know who will be true
My someone who will never let me be blue
This true love I have found in you
This cat will forever love you
You are my life, my everything
I love when you say tell me something
Your finger I want to place that ring
I love all your little things

Thank you
Thank you for being such a monster,
Making me feel like I had nothing to offer,
For making me believe I needed a doctor,
For being a frequent "shopper".
For making yourself unclear,
Giving the impression I was the reason you
threw back the beer
For making love my number one fear,
And never wiping my endless tears.
Thank you for making your love a lie,
Never giving me a fair try,
Saying things that made me want to die,
For never giving me a proper goodbye,
Using me just to get by,
For making me feel like I was a waste of your
time
Leaving me to wonder why
Damn you, for all the sleepless nights
Thank you for all the off and on I'm in love
with you speech
For making me your fucking leech
For the regret of love not inside of you, I
desperately tried to seek
Making me feel like a tasteless piece of meat.
Thank you for making my heart heavy as lead,
For constantly fucking with my head,
Never meaning you loved me when you said,
For being so full of shit,
Only giving me a little bit,
Making me believe I couldn't quit.
Thank you for leaving a bitter taste in my
mouth
Leaving your poisonous stinger I cannot get
out,
Keeping my mind in doubt,
Never hearing my silent shouts.
Thank you for driving me mad,
Being the reason our "relationship" went bad
Treating me like a fad,

Never giving a damn that you made me sad
Thank you for making your comments snide
For never being satisfied,
Saying shit just to pacify,
For making me endure painful sights.
Thank you for making me feel like a disease,
Keeping me on my bruised knees,
Being so blind to my love that you overseen,
Never wanting to set me free.
Thank you for making me feel transparent
For being so self-absorbent
Making me believe you were all for it
For loving all the others damn it
Thank you for being so contradictive,
For remaining vindictive,
Giving up and not telling me when you did
For your dirtiness I cannot rid.
Thank you for being so confusing,
Thanks for all the mental abusing,
For my love that you continued using,
Making me feel like I was never amusing.
Thank you for making me feel hideous
Never taking us serious,
Making my mind delirious,
Putting on that front, so I could not see you are
deleterious.
Thank you for making me a blank page in your book,
For getting me hooked,
Never giving me a second look,
Never thinking twice about the chance you should
have took.
Mostly thank you for helping me realize that I can cut
so deep,
To where it's just your poison that from my veins it
seeps,
Thank you for helping me see,
That you are incredibly weak,
For all that I now know, it's you I can defeat,
It's you, I no longer need.

Lying here with you

This is where I felt my lowest low
Right beneath this old weeping willow
The memories that would sink in
For days left my eyes stingin'
Driving away for the first time
I just couldn't seem to get you off my mind
Looking in my rearview, I'd sigh
Seeing flashbacks of you and I
I know this love gets tough sometimes
But that doesn't mean in my heart you're not
still mine
When I toss and turn at night
You're the only one I want holding me tight
Cuz' when I saw you I knew
I found my home lying here with you
We would waste cold days away lying in your
bed
When the sun would peak through, it would
dance upon your head
Those beautiful sun rays would make the
perfect halo
You'd smile at me, I knew I found my angel
I would do anything you asked me to
Hell and high water I would tread through
No one is ever going to get me like you do
It's you, they could never amount to
I know this love gets tough sometimes
But that doesn't mean in my heart you're not
still mine
And when I toss and turn at night
You're the only one I want holding me tight
Cuz' when I saw you I knew
I found my home lying here with you
You can call me crazy
I knew you'd find your way back to me baby
No matter how far the rage pushes us in this
sea
I know one thing for sure, you belong here
with me

It's been years since we spoke
So I'll try to get this right without the choke
Your hands are still warm like I remember
Like that cold night in December
I can't take one more day without you in it
To start anew, I'm more than willin'
I just want you with me dear
And now it's never been clearer
I love you, I've waited so long to once again
hear
I know this love gets tough sometimes
But to me you have always been mine
You're the one that has my heart
You always have, right from the start
Cuz' when I saw you I knew
I found my home lying here with you
Yeah, I'm at home now, lying here with you

Bombshell

To my eyes you're so pleasin'
Baby there are a million reasons
It's your humor I'm fienin'
There is more to you than everyone is seein'
These fools are not treating you right
You need the realness of me in your life
It's not that you are known internationally
Or that you are stunning externally
It's because the nature of your originality
Is deeply rooted with your majestic personality
That chance with you is a long shot
But I will give it all I got
Back in the day
I loved your rocker chick phase
Girl that was my fav
That guitar you would play
How aggressive you were on that stage
I'd smile at the things you would say
Damn, how your voice dominates
My stress, it eliminates
Tell me it's in the cards
That I could hold the key to your heart
Babe from day one
You had this cat sprung
The way you would chew your gum
To every song that was sung
How flawless your hair looked in that bun
It's a fact, we would have a lot of fun
You just seem so down to earth
How real you are with every verse
It turns me on when you curse
You shine so bright like a sunburst
Let me say that smile
Makes my heart go wild
Your unique style
Anything looks good that you compile
When I close my eyes I can picture this

You sittin' there in that red velvet dress
Putting on that diamond necklace
Those curls look so at rest
Gently brush your hair to one side of your shoulders
As you seductively look me over
Biting that bottom lip
Come here love, give me a kiss
Trace your every curve with my fingertips
Pull you closer by your hips
Whisper these dirty words in your ear like a script
Grab your thighs and give you a lift
Comfortably on my waist you sit
I love how deep that V is between your tits
That heavy stare
Putting on that pressure
I'm thinking I need to undress her
Lay you on that silk comforter
Or love, if you're just up for conversatin'
Then we can wait on these temptations
You are something definitely worth waitin'
Memorable moments we can start makin'
No need for rushin'
I like the slow touchin'
Baby you have me crushin'
And I have you blushin'
This glow is so stunnin'
Everything you are, I'm lovin'
We could chill watching Netflix
Maybe sneak in a little kiss
Feed you those cookies with the mint
Brand me with your fingerprints
Anything you want miss
I'm up for it

Rearview

You say come with me and stay the night,
 I promise to hold you tight.
Together we spend the days and so many nights,
Not letting each other out of sight.
The more time spent, the more our feelings grew.
I can't believe I found someone as special as you.
You say you love my hair, love my style, and can't
wait to see my smile.
The feeling I get when I'm with you makes every
second worthwhile.
Damn baby I love your smile, it drives me absolutely
wild.
But as time passes by, the way you changed I could
tell.
By looking in your eyes there was someone else
Why did you have to go? You tell me you got scared?
What the hell! To be with you I'm putting everything
on the line here!
Was my first move too late? Or was this a decision
you had already made.
Thanks for throwing the flowers back in my face.
Now I know pain has a taste.
You're making me bitter not sweet but cold.
I hope you know people like you are alone when they
grow old.
I should have known better you're a fucking tease!
I'm just one of the losers in your game that you seize.
You ripped my heart open wide and made me change
what I felt inside.
Yes it is you I once adored, now those feelings are
gone, I have no more.
But what did I tell you before, don't say feelings if
they aren't really there.
You tell me you miss me , you love me, and even act
like you care.
Is that all I was, a challenge for you?
Give you my all and now we're through.
You little mother fucker! I can't believe I loved you!

I hope one day you will open your eyes and see, how much you did mean to me.

You blew me kisses, gave me hugs, made it seem like you were very much in love.

I just wish I would have known that stuff was to make it tough.

Now I hate your smile, I hate your eyes, and hate the way you make me feel inside.

Go ahead tell me more lies, I know you get off on seeing cry

Is this shit to much? Am I making it hard?

Well suck it up because you broke my fucking heart!

You'll be sorry when I'm gone,

That's when our "friendship" will no longer be strong.

When conversations are short, sweet, and to the point.

A quick hello, how are you, and goodnight.

But it's ok and it's alright.

Someday I will find someone that reminds me nothing of you,

And you will just be a forgotten memory in my fucking rearview.

www.ingramcontent.com/pod-product-compliance
Lightning Source LLC
Chambersburg PA
CBHW060950040426
42445CB00011B/1092